My Little Golden Book About
GREEK GODS
AND GODDESSES

By John Sazaklis

Illustrated by Elsa Chang

The editors would like to thank John Jay Professor Deborah Steiner
of the Department of Classics at Columbia University for her assistance
in the preparation of this book.

A GOLDEN BOOK • NEW YORK

Educators and librarians, for a variety of teaching tools, visit us at RHTeachersLibrarians.com
Library of Congress Control Number: 2021943284
ISBN 978-0-593-42739-2 (trade) — ISBN 978-0-593-42740-8 (ebook)
Printed in the United States of America
10 9 8 7 6 5 4 3

Long ago, the ancient Greeks believed in magical beings called gods and goddesses. These beings controlled all parts of life, such as nature, the weather, and even death.

The most powerful gods and goddesses were the Olympians. They lived on Mount Olympus— the highest mountaintop in all of Greece.

Reading about the gods and goddesses teaches us a lot about Greek history. For example, the country's capital, Athens, was named after the goddess Athena.

ATHENA (uh-THEE-nuh)

Athena was the goddess of battle and wisdom. She helped heroes win wars and taught the people many crafts, such as spinning thread and weaving. Weaving is the art of making fabric by interlacing threads of yarn or other materials.

ZEUS (ZOOS)

Athena's father, Zeus, ruled the skies as the king of Olympus. He could zap lightning bolts at anyone and anything that made him angry. The Greeks believed thunderstorms were caused by his bad temper.

HERA (HEH-ruh)

Ruling next to Zeus was Hera, the queen of Olympus. Hera was the goddess of marriage. She married Zeus in a magical garden where the trees grew golden apples that made anyone who ate them live forever. Hera guarded the garden with the help of a dangerous dragon!

POSEIDON (poh-SY-duhn)

Zeus had a brother named Poseidon. This water-controlling warrior was the god of the seas and oceans. He rode the waves while wielding his terrific trident. This three-pointed spear could create sea storms and earthquakes!

Poseidon and Athena held a contest to see who could give the best gift to what would become the city of Athens. Poseidon's gifts—the horse and the saltwater stream—were useful, but Athena's gift—the olive tree—gave shade, shelter, and food. Athena was declared the winner, and Athens got its name.

DEMETER (duh-ME-ter)

Hera's sister Demeter was the goddess of the harvest. She spent time on Earth teaching humans how to plant and grow crops. The weather changed depending on her moods—this explained the changing of the seasons.

PERSEPHONE (per-SEH-fuh-nee)

Persephone was Demeter's daughter, the goddess of spring and the queen of the underworld, where ancient Greeks believed their souls went after they died. While Persephone was ruling the land of the dead, her mother's sadness stopped the crops from growing. When Persephone returned, her mother's joy turned the weather warm and nature bloomed again.

HADES (HAY-deez)

This gloomy god was Zeus's brother and the lord of the underworld. His palace was guarded by Cerberus, a hungry three-headed dog!

HESTIA (HES-tee-uh)

Hera's sister Hestia was the goddess of the hearth, or fireplace. It was her duty to watch over households and teach people how to bake bread. Every home used its hearth as a place to pray to Hestia.

APOLLO (uh-PAH-loh)

Apollo was the god of music, poetry, and art. He loved to play the lyre—a stringed instrument made from a tortoise shell. Apollo had healing powers and could help people see the future. His twin sister was the goddess Artemis.

ARTEMIS (AR-teh-mis)

Skilled with a bow and arrow, Artemis was the goddess of the hunt and the protector of young women. She liked living in the forest instead of on Mount Olympus. Many female athletes competed in races, dances, and games to honor Artemis.

APHRODITE (a-fro-DY-tee)

Aphrodite, the goddess of love, was born fully grown from the foam of the sea. She was also the goddess of beauty. She made gods as well as humans fall in love, with help from her son Eros . . . and his magical arrows!

ARES (AIR-eez)

Ares was a son of Zeus and Hera. He was the god of war—and the most unpopular of all the Olympians. Always dressed in armor, Ares liked to fight. He even created an army of women warriors named the Amazons!

HERMES (HER-meez)

Swift and sneaky Hermes was the god of thieves. He was a prankster who could travel at superspeed with his winged helmet and sandals. His father, Zeus, put him to work as the messenger of the gods.

HEPHAESTUS (hy-FEH-stus)

Hephaestus was Hera's son and a blacksmith. He made weapons and armor for warriors. It was believed that his workshops were inside volcanoes, and that when Hephaestus was hard at work, the volcanoes would erupt. *KA-BOOM!*

DIONYSUS (DY-uh-NY-suss)

One of the youngest Olympians was Dionysus.
He loved living in nature and taught people how
to use grapes to make wine. He was the god of
winemaking, the theater, and parties.

THE OLYMPIANS LOVED PARTIES!

The ancient Greeks held a special festival to honor the gods and goddesses. The festival took place every four years in the city of Olympia. Athletes would compete at the temple of Zeus in many events, such as running, jumping, wrestling, the discus throw, and the chariot race.

Three thousand years later, the Olympic Games
are still held, all around the world!

The Greek gods and goddesses can be found all around us—not only in their ancient temples and museums, but in our constellations, movies, games, and more. Keep your eyes peeled . . . you never know where you might see them!